The Penknife

Written by Nigel Watts
Illustrated by Anna C. Leplar

Collins Educational

An Imprint of HarperCollins*Publishers*

Chapter One

The day was ruined. Evan and Jake had enjoyed themselves fishing, even though they hadn't caught anything. And then Evan found his penknife had gone. He searched his pockets and his fishing box. Nothing. He looked on the ground where they had been sitting. Nothing. He tried not to cry as he searched his pockets again.

His penknife was his most precious possession.

"My grandad gave it to me before he died," he blurted. "It's an antique."

Jake knew all about the knife. He had seen it lots of times before. It was the most beautiful thing he had ever seen. Its blade was solid silver and its handle was made of ebony. Evan said it was worth hundreds of pounds.

Now he had lost it.

They spent half an hour searching the river bank, but they couldn't find the knife. Jake's dad drove them home in silence. Evan was sitting in the back, crying. It was a disaster.

Evan broke the silence. "Somebody must have stolen it," he said.

"Who?" Jake could feel the hairs prickle on the back of his neck, but he didn't turn round.

"Those boys who looked through my fishing tackle. I bet it was them."

Jake remembered the boys, bullies from the middle school. "Maybe."

"Who else could it have been?" Evan asked.

"I don't know."

"You should tell your father," Jake's dad said. "There's too much stealing going on."

Evan's dad was a policeman. Evan had brought his dad's truncheon to school one day and got into trouble.

They dropped Evan off at his home. Evan looked very glum.

That night when Jake was in bed and the light was off, he reached into his jeans pocket and pulled out a knife. A penknife with a carved ebony handle and a silver blade. He held it up to the street light and turned the blade so light flickered across his face. He shouldn't have stolen it, he knew. But it was so beautiful.

Chapter Two

Evan was upset all the next day. He sat through Maths with his head in his hands, not even trying to answer the questions. At playtime he didn't join in the game of rounders. Jake was supposed to be Evan's best friend, but today Jake was making friends with Martin. He pretended not to notice Evan in the corner of the playground.

When Evan knocked over a pot of water in Art, Miss Barnett called him to the front.

"Is something wrong, Evan?" she asked.

"Someone has stolen my knife, Miss."

"Not the silver knife with the ebony handle?"

Everyone in the class had seen the penknife. He had brought it in one day and Miss Barnett had allowed the children to pass it round.

"Yes," said Evan, quietly.

The teacher noticed that Jake was watching them so she called him over.

"Evan is upset. I'd like you two to work together."

"Do we have to, Miss?" Jake said.

"I thought you were best friends?" Jake said nothing and Evan looked hurt.

The class was making a model of a
medieval village, so Evan helped Jake
with the castle. They hardly said
anything to each other. When Evan
cut the wrong piece of cardboard by
mistake, Jake got angry.

"Stupid!" he tutted.

"I'm not."

"Of course you are. You wouldn't
lose your knife otherwise."

"I didn't lose it. Somebody stole it."

"No they didn't. You lost it. I bet you dropped it in the river."

"I didn't!"

"Stop squabbling, you two," Miss Barnett called out, "or I'll split you up."

"Good," Jake muttered.

The two boys said nothing to each other for the rest of the day.

At the end of the day Jake
waited in the classroom until Evan
had left. He didn't want to walk home
with him.

Jake felt ashamed of stealing the
knife. He was so ashamed that now he
was making his best friend an enemy.
He could never admit to Evan what
he had done. He walked home alone,
confused and angry.

Chapter Three

Jake knew he was in trouble as soon as he saw his parents' faces. They were sitting at the kitchen table, waiting for him. The penknife was on the table between them. Jake saw it straight away.

"Well?" his dad asked.

Jake couldn't think of anything to say. There was a heavy silence.

"You stole it, then?" his dad continued.

"No."

"So, how did it get under your pillow?" his mum asked.

"I don't know," he said weakly.

His dad stood up and gave the penknife to Jake. "You're going to take this round to Evan right now. Get in the car and wait for me."

Jake did as he was told. Amanda, his older sister, followed him out of the house. She looked scared and excited at the same time.

Jake wound the window down so she could talk to him.

"You're in big trouble," Amanda threatened.

"I know."

"Let's hope Evan's dad won't press charges," she said.

"Press charges?" Jake said in a small voice. "What's that?"

"Arrest you."

Jake felt sick. He wound the window up and Amanda went inside.

"Arrest me?" he thought. Could the police arrest someone who was only nine? He wasn't going to stay to find out. He opened the car door and got out.

He started walking quickly down the road. Then he started trotting, then running, then sprinting.

He ran to the wood, to the old oak tree. A rope ladder hung down its trunk and he climbed up until he reached the tree house. He pulled the rope ladder up behind him and tugged the door into place. He was safe for the moment.

Jake was so scared he couldn't think straight. If Evan's dad arrested him, would they send him to prison? Perhaps a children's prison was like an orphanage. He had seen pictures of an old orphanage. It had high windows so you couldn't look out, and the children slept in dormitories.

"I would rather live in a tree house than go to prison," he said to himself.

He had made the tree house last summer with Evan. They had found some old planks and, with a bit of help from Evan's mum, they had made it safe and strong. They had put an old cot mattress in it and nailed bits of carpet to the sides. A proper door with hinges had been made, and a padlock kept people out. Everyone was jealous of their tree house, but only special guests were allowed up.

The wood was quiet and, after his heart had stopped thumping, Jake opened the door an inch. He liked this wood. He and Evan had played here since they were little. They had chosen this oak tree for the tree house because it had always been their favourite. It was here that Evan first showed him the penknife, just after his grandad had died. Jake took the penknife out of his pocket and opened it up.

He wished he hadn't stolen it now. But it was too late. He had stolen it, and now he had been found out.

After about an hour had passed, he heard the sound of crashing through the undergrowth. He shut the door quickly and then peered through a crack in the floorboards. It was his dad.

"Jacob. Are you up there?"

His dad only called him Jacob when he was in trouble. Jake said nothing.

"I know you're up there," his dad called. "Come down." He sounded very angry.

Jake held his breath, willing his dad to go away. He could see him staring up at the tree, his hand shading his eyes. His dad waited for a few minutes, then strode away through the undergrowth and it was quiet again.

Chapter Four

The wood was different in the dark. It wasn't friendly any more. The outline of branches against the sky looked like arms. Things rustled in the undergrowth. Jake tried not to think of ghosts and monsters.

His eyes were aching from trying to see in the dusk.

The moon kept disappearing and reappearing from behind the clouds, making shadows dance. Suddenly something swooped towards him and he leapt backwards with a shout. A dark shape brushed against his face and he swiped at it. Then he heard high-pitched squeaking. Bats. He shuddered.

It was all too much for him. He let down the rope ladder and climbed down. Perhaps Evan wouldn't tell his dad after all, and he wouldn't be arrested and sent away.

He ran through the wood and the faster he ran, the more scared he was. He imagined the trees were trying to grab him, the roots trying to trip him up. He heard something scream in the darkness – a fox calling for her cubs.

It was only when he reached the street lights that he stopped to catch his breath. The streets were deserted. Everybody was indoors watching television or having dinner. The houses looked cosy with their curtains drawn and their lights on. He felt safe again.

When he reached his house the kitchen was dark, so he let himself in by the back door. He was starving. He took a chicken leg from the fridge and ate it so quickly he almost choked. He thought about going up to bed, going to sleep and pretending nothing had happened. Maybe he would wake in the morning and it would be another day and he wouldn't be in trouble and Evan would still have his knife.

His hand was on the kitchen door when he heard his dad's voice.

He was speaking on the phone.

"Yes, Mr Morris, I agree. I think it's too late to get him down now. I'll go back in the morning. Then we can decide what to do with him."

Mr Morris was Evan's dad. Chief Inspector Morris. What would they *do* with him? Jake remembered the long black truncheon, how heavy it had felt. He shut the door quietly.

He emptied the contents of the biscuit tin into his pockets, took an apple from the bowl and crept out of the house. The dark was frightening, but not as frightening as going to prison.

There was only one place to go, so he ran back to the tree and climbed up the ladder. It was cold now. He wished he had brought his coat.

He ate all the biscuits, one after another, until they were all gone. He felt sick.

He took the penknife out of his pocket. He wished he had never seen Evan's stupid knife. He opened the door and threw it as far as he could out into the dark. It landed somewhere in the bushes.

Eventually he drifted off to sleep. A restless sleep filled with dreams of policemen and prisons.

Chapter Five

He felt stiff when he woke up and his teeth were furry because he hadn't cleaned them. Something was tickling his ear and he pulled a beetle out of his hair. He had rolled off the mattress in the night, and his clothes were rust-coloured with sawdust.

"What shall I do now?" he said to himself. "If I don't go to school, I'll be in even bigger trouble. But if I go, I'll have to admit to Evan I stole his knife."

Just then he heard the bushes rustling and caught snatches of voices he recognised. He strained to listen.

"Let me talk to him, John," he heard. It was his mum. He peered through the crack at her. He had to gulp back tears when he saw her.

He was suddenly homesick.

"Jake," she called. "We know you're up there. Come on down, darling. Please."

There was a long pause. It was very tempting.

"Evan knows you've got his knife. If you just give it back to him, I'm sure he'll forgive you," she said.

But he didn't have the knife any more! It was somewhere in the bushes. It might be lost!

"If you don't come down on your own," – it was his dad's voice and he sounded angry – "we'll have to get you down ourselves."

There was the sound of rattling and Jake saw a ladder appear. It didn't reach the platform. He could hear the sound of his dad climbing the ladder. He could hear him grunting with the effort.

He was almost at the top when there was a cry and then a crash. The ladder slipped and he fell into the bushes.

Jake opened the door and looked down. His dad was lying on his side, moaning in pain. "I think I've broken my leg," he groaned.

Jake's mum helped him to his feet. Even from high above their heads, Jake could see his dad's face was white with pain. He hobbled away, supported on one side by Jake's mum.

"Now look what I've done," Jake muttered tearfully. He was getting deeper and deeper into trouble.

He sat in the tree house all afternoon, not knowing what to do. His father would be in hospital now, having a plaster cast put on his leg. Evan would probably never speak to him again.

And the police – with all their sirens and dogs and handcuffs – were sure to come sooner or later.

"Are you up there?" A loud voice suddenly broke into his thoughts. Jake didn't answer. Startled, he looked down to see two firefighters propping a ladder up against the tree.

A minute later, there was a knock on the door. "Come on laddie, let us in," one of the firefighters called.

Jake was too frightened to speak.

"You know, we've rescued cats from trees," the firefighter continued through the door, "and boys from burning buildings. Even cats from burning buildings. But *never* a boy from a tree."

Jake liked the sound of the man. He sounded friendly.

"I can't come down," Jake said at last.

"I'm in too much trouble."

"*Nobody's* in too much trouble," the firefighter continued.

"I am."

"What have you done wrong?" the firefighter asked.

"I can't tell you."

"Yes, you can."

"I'm ashamed to," Jake said.

There was a long pause.

"If you don't come out son, I'm afraid we'll have to break the door down."

"No, please don't," Jake said quietly.

"Will you come down on your own?"

Jake blocked his ears so he couldn't hear any more.

A few minutes later he realised the firefighters had gone.

The day wore on. There was
nothing to do except doze. Late in the
afternoon, Jake opened the door and
had a stretch. Then he saw something
at the bottom of the tree. It looked
like food.

He checked to see that there was
nobody around, then he dropped the
rope ladder and climbed down.

Somebody had left some sandwiches, a torch and a blanket he didn't recognise. Jake went to the toilet and then climbed back into the tree house with his supplies.

He ate the sandwiches at what he guessed was teatime. The sun started to set soon afterwards, and Jake lay down on the mattress. The torch batteries didn't last long, but he was so tired he fell asleep before it was completely dark.

Chapter Six

"Jacob Green?"

Jake woke up with a start. It was morning, and someone was calling his name. He rubbed the sleep from his eyes and peered through the crack in the floor. Two police officers and his mum were staring up at the tree. There was also a boy with them.

Jake realised with a shock that it was Evan. Then he recognised one of the police officers. It was Evan's dad, Chief Inspector Morris.

"Come on down, Jake. Enough is enough," his mum called. "You'll only get into more trouble if you stay up there."

"I'm already in enough trouble," Jake said quietly. "I don't want to be arrested and taken to prison."

"If you don't come down Jacob, we'll have to break the tree house apart," Evan's dad said. The constable with him held up a crowbar and a hammer.

"But Dad!" Jake heard Evan say, "You can't do that."

"I'm sorry, Evan. It's the only way," his dad said.

The constable put a ladder against the tree trunk and began to climb.

She held the crowbar and hammer in one hand.

"First my penknife, and now our tree house," Evan protested. "It's not fair!"

Suddenly Jake knew what he had to do. He opened the door and lowered the rope ladder. The police officer paused and then looked at Chief Inspector Morris. Evan's dad told the constable to come back down.

"Evan. Will you come up?" Jake called.

Evan climbed up the rope ladder. Jake helped him into the tree house and then shut the door.

"I'm coming down," Jake said. "I won't let them break up our tree house."

"Good," said Evan.

There was a long pause while Jake fidgeted.

"I'm sorry for stealing your knife," he said at last. He could feel his face redden.

Evan shrugged. "I was really angry, but I'm not any more. Where is it?"

"It's somewhere in the bushes. We can find it though," he added quickly. "Is your dad going to arrest me now?"

"Of course not."

"I won't go to prison?"

"Children don't go to prison. And anyway, who goes to prison for borrowing a penknife?"

"But – "

"You're my best friend, Jake. I'm not going to get you into trouble." Evan picked up the torch and clicked it on and off. "The batteries are dead," he murmured.

Jake suddenly realised who had brought the food and blanket. It was Evan.

"Thanks," Jake said. He felt ashamed of treating his friend so badly, but glad he had owned up. He took a deep breath and opened the door.

"I'm coming down." Everyone breathed a *huge* sigh of relief.

Jake's mum wanted to take him home straight away, but Jake insisted that they look for the penknife. It was only a few minutes before the police constable found it in a patch of stinging nettles. "Here it is!" she cried. Evan took the penknife and wiped it clean. He put it in his pocket with a smile.

"Now, how are we going to deal with you, young man?" Jake's mum said to him.

Chief Inspector Morris stepped forward. He looked very important in his police uniform with silver buttons. "I think two days in a tree is enough of a punishment, don't you?"

He brushed some of the sawdust out of Jake's hair.

"What this boy needs, more than anything, is a good bath."